The Passionate Heart

The Passionate Heart

Sacred Poetry For The Heart

Dhanook Singh

To order additional copies of this book, contact:
Xlibris Corporation
1-888-795-4274
www.Xlibris.com
Orders@Xlibris.com
85599

Dedication

To my wife Loretta J. McAvoy whose love and

immense support is deeply appreciated. You are my

beloved and my teacher.

Acknowledgements

"Step over the edge / dare to be insane / see the unseen / fall deeply / madly in love" captures the journey this book represents. There have been many starts and stops but, in the end, many insights. I wish to thank all my teachers from the many personal growth courses I have taken over the years.

A special thank-you to my spiritual teacher and fellow poet Jeffrey Armstrong and his wife Sandi Graham, for providing the Thank Goddess It's Friday (TGIF) gatherings where I had an opportunity to read my poetry to an array of people. Jeffrey encouraged me and insisted that I have a writer in me that needed to be expressed.

Thank you to Julie Blue and the choir from 1997 and 1998, for outing me as a poet. You gave me the opportunity to share my poetry for the first time by allowing me to read at our concerts. I remember one member took my first handwritten poetry book and typing it up.

Satyen Raja, thank you, for pushing me to grow and seeing the power of my heart. Our Spiritual Adventure Tour of India was a journey into my own heart and a dance with my ancestors.

Thank you to Rosemary Thomlinson-Morris for being my first muse. We met some twenty-eight years ago at university. What great fun, pain, love, and joy we have shared over the years. You, your husband Martin, and family will always have a special place in my heart

My friend Alida Van Braeden, who also journeyed through India with us, thank you for helping me with the initial editing.

To my family in the Toronto area, thank you for the lessons in life. I have deep gratitude to my mother, Pamela for all the sacrifices she made for my sisters, brother, and I. You are the strongest woman I know.

Finally, to my beloved Loretta McAvoy, thank you for all your support and encouragement. Thank you for keeping the home front going while I worked on this project on weekends.

Contents

Die With Me

Die in my arms;
I will die in yours.

Are you willing to DIE
In order to live?

I am afraid of this journey
For I know the end.

Am I ready
To live the death of life?

Is this the day?
Is it tomorrow?

I am committed to doing things differently.
Will you help me drink the nectar?

Let us be children
And run naked in the rain;
Stick our tongues out and taste the raindrops.

Let us be songbirds
And sing as loud as we can;
Notes don't matter when you sing from the heart.

Let us be giddy newborns
And discover gravity all over again;
Fall down and laugh for no reason at all.

Let us drink each other's eyes
And listen, truly listen;
Skip the small talk:
Talk about what matters most to you.

Let us learn how to die
So we can learn how to live;
Drink every drop.
Savor every ray of sunshine;
Inhale the fragrances all around us:
Be the beauty.

Don't wait;
Die with me today.

Let us play in the garden
And be drunk with life.

August 12, 2006
Inspired after seeing a play
based on the book Tuesdays with Morrie

December 2005. The cemetery in Havana, Cuba.

How to Read an Echo Poem

Four people, as "echoes," are required. One person stands in each of the four corners of the room. The reader reads a line and then directs each of the "echoes" who in turn repeats the echo line. So, for example, the reader reads the first line, then echo 1 repeats the echo line, then echo 2, and so on. This gives the listeners a 3-D stereo effect.

Flow

An Echo Poem

I am the leaf upon the tree
Echo   *Leaf upon the tree*
       Leaf upon the tree
       Leaf upon the tree
       Leaf upon the tree
Falling in the wind
Becoming the root
Becoming the tree
Becoming the wind

I am the breath upon the wind
Echo   *Breath upon the wind*
       Breath upon the wind
       Breath upon the wing
       Breath upon the wing
Rising in the clouds
Becoming the rains
Becoming the seas
Becoming the tears

I am the boy within the man
Echo   *Boy within the man*
       Boy within the man
       Boy within the man
       Boy within the man
Learning in life
Becoming the warrior
Becoming the wizard
Becoming the king

She is the girl within the woman
Echo   *Girl within the woman*
         Girl within the woman
         Girl within the woman
         Girl within the woman
         Growing in beauty
Becoming the Priestess
Becoming the Wild Woman
Becoming the Madonna

I am the cell within her body
Echo   *Cell within her body*
         Cell within her body
         Cell within her body
         Cell within her body
Moving in the web
Becoming the body
Becoming the corpse
Becoming the leaf

January 2000
After my first ten-day silent
Vipassana meditation
January 2000

August 2007. Puddle on the jungle floor on a walk through the tropical rainforest in Guyana.

Dragon by the Sea

An Echo Poem

Oh to be a dragon by the sea
Echo   *Oh to be a dragon by the sea*
         Oh to be a dragon by the sea
         Oh to be a dragon by the sea
         Oh to be a dragon by the sea
To know the law of pure potentiality
To make all possibilities our reality

Oh to be a dragon by the sea
Echo   *Oh to be a dragon by the sea*
         Oh to be a dragon by the sea
         Oh to be a dragon by the sea
         Oh to be a dragon by the sea
To circulate the abundance of the universe
To give and receive in dynamic equilibrium

Oh to be a dragon by the sea
Echo   *Oh to be a dragon by the sea*
         Oh to be a dragon by the sea
         Oh to be a dragon by the sea
         Oh to be a dragon by the sea
To tune in to nature's intelligence
To effortlessly harness the forces of joy and harmony

Oh to be a dragon by the sea
Echo   *Oh to be a dragon by the sea*
         Oh to be a dragon by the sea
         Oh to be a dragon by the sea
         Oh to be a dragon by the sea
To plant our desires in the field of pure potentiality
To live in the wisdom of uncertainty

Oh to be a dragon by the sea
Echo   *Oh to be a dragon by the sea*
        Oh to be a dragon by the sea
        Oh to be a dragon by the sea
        Oh to be a dragon by the sea
To live the freedom of detachment
To reap the karma of what we sow

Oh to be a dragon by the sea
Echo   *Oh to be a dragon by the sea*
        Oh to be a dragon by the sea
        Oh to be a dragon by the sea
        Oh to be a dragon by the sea
To know the exultation of our own spirit
To selflessly give our unique gift to the universe

Oh to be a dragon by the sea
Echo   *Oh to be a dragon by the sea*
        Oh to be a dragon by the sea
        Oh to be a dragon by the sea
        Oh to be a dragon by the sea

Inspired by Deepak Chopra's book
Seven Laws of Spiritual Success

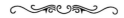

March 2008. Brown pelicans near the fishing village of Puerto Morelos, Mexico.

The warrior moved with subtle
beauty as he prepared himself.
There was a fluid symmetry to his movement;
his strength was like metal,
yet his energy shifted and changed.

He used his energy wisely:
the only battle that mattered
was inside rather than outside.

He noticed the buds on the trees in the garden.
The songs of the birds crested his ears.
His nostrils drank the warm scented breeze.
Sweet cherry water danced in his mouth.
The air was an extension of his tanned skin.

In a peaceful garden a lone warrior prepared.
Life was being created, preserved, and destroyed,
only to begin again.
His preparation were almost complete.

How would he teach
the children about beauty and strength?

July 1998

January 2009. A yogi who is the keeper of the Shiva Fire that has burned
continuously for more than five thousand years at Varanasi, India. The
Shiva Fire is used to light all cremation fires beside the sacred Ganges river.

Beauty lives in fields of flowers
Beauty lives on mountaintops
Beauty is not found in a jar
Beauty is not found on a magazine cover
Beauty lives in the heart
Beauty lives in the spirit
I see beauty in you

1997

August 2010. The view from the Banff Springs Hotel in Banff, Alberta.

Earth
You are sacred wine
Sweet, fragrant
Served at the feast

Air
You are wildflowers
Bright, sensual
Growing high above the field

Water
You are springwaters
Alive, nourishing
Flowing to the sea

Fire
You are the stone
Strong, pitted
Glowing in the fire

1997

January 2009. The amazing Taj Mahal, India, reflected in the courtyard pool.

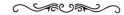

Hold my hand and walk with me
Walk with me through alpine meadows
Walk with me through burning deserts
Hold my hand and feel the rain
Hold my hand and feel the wind

1997

November 2009. Our friends Jo and Mike Chevin holding hands at a dinner party.

Goddess of the Night

I have a new lover tonight.
Her voice is soft,
her caress silky,
her lips like nectar
from a field of wildflowers.

She speaks to me in the night,
telling me about Australopithecus, Cro-Magnon,
four-legged becoming two,
fires of iron and bronze,
leaps of faith and science.

My new lover is never content,
loving me through the night.
My passion makes her want more,
more of me each night
until we melt.

We melt sweetly,
remembering Plato and Romeo.
We kiss, tenderly
honoring Aphrodite and Cleopatra.
Ah! The ecstasy.

Each night we meet in the light.
You know her too, goddess of the night.
She is there, full, waiting
for lovers without a love.

March 9, 2001

January 2009. The sunset over the western mosque at the Taj Mahal, India.

Eyes

Into golden fragrant pools
I swim wingless
flying deep
deep down
following spirits of essence

I cannot see
for I have no eyes
yet I am present
gathering the sweet mysteries of life

I cannot speak
for I have no voice
yet I am present
moving down the tree of life

I cannot walk
for I have no feet
yet I am present
enacting the timeless rhythm of life

I cannot touch
for I have no arms
yet I am present
swimming deep
deep down
into golden pools of essence

March 28, 2001

January 2009. A Berber-looking man at the Shiva Fire at Varanasi, India.

Shadow of My Light

For a girlfriend with leukemia

Thank you for showing me my light
You live in the glow of an x-ray
You dance with the wild cells
You dread tasting my chemo-cocktail

Thank you for showing me my courage
You know the jab of needles
You know the sick smell of hospitals
You know my cries of pain

Thank you for showing me
My love of life
My love of family
My human mortality

Now I know my light
It is my quiet strength
It is my inner beauty
It is always lives in my heart

Shadow of my light
I wish you would be gone
I don't always understand
I want to know why

I'm afraid
Shadow of my light
Please teach me

May 1999

August 2007. Sunset from my uncle's boat on the Pomeroon River, Guyana, where my father's family first settled.

Mantra of the Spiritual Warrior

Be without fear in the face of your demons;
embrace and accept your shadow.

Be brave and upright so the divine may love you;
see the divine everywhere.

Speak your truth always, even if it leads to your death;
speak the bigger truths of life.

Safeguard the helpless and be in service;
strive to make a difference in the world.

Cultivate your consciousness;
plant seeds of transformation.

Love deeply with all of your soul;
have courage and open your heart.

July 5, 2006
Inspired by the movie *Kingdom of Heaven*

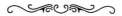

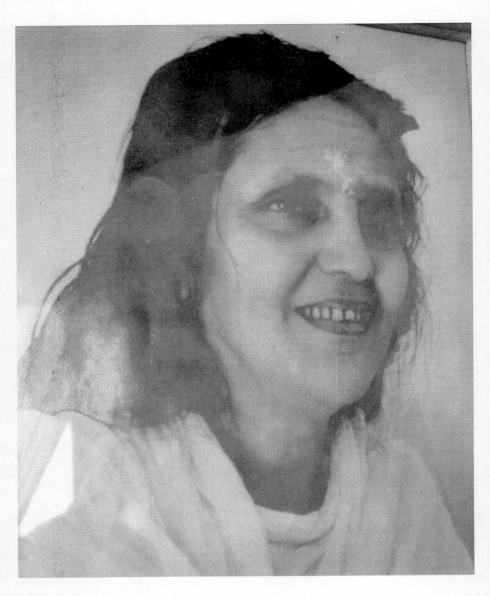

January 2009. Sri Anandamayi Ma, a Hindu spiritual teacher and guru
that resided in a simple room and was a teacher for the Maharaja of
Tehri-Garhwal at his place in Rishikesh, India. Part of the palace is now a
beautiful ayurveda spa in the foothills of the Himalayas.

Tree within the Seed

I am the tree within the seed
hungry for the food you feed me,
alive in the divine—
what messages do you have?

I am the butterfly within the cocoon.
Tell me your dreams.
The universe rests on your desire—
tune in now.

I am the embryo within the womb,
sleeping in light.
Swim with me—
the possibilities are limitless.

I am Shakti and Shiva in the eye of the needle—
step into the centre.
Do for the good of all.
Become the Buddha, self-aware.

I am your thoughts within cosmic consciousness—
speak and be heard.
Ask and be loved.
Open and be seen.
You are the tree within the seed.

July 5, 2000

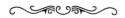

January 2009. The Bodhi Tree where Buddha became enlightened at Bodhgaya, India. The Bodhi tree dies then regrows. This Bodhi tree is a pilgrimage site for Buddhists worldwide.

To Love

When I was in love with you
it was madness;
the earth erupted
and then subsided.
My roots struggled to hold the ground.

I was drunk with you.
Feeling the sky, I woke up.
Is love being breathless?
Is love the excitement?
Is love the desire?

The desire to make love with you every second of the day,
the desire to kiss every part of your body,
the desire to tingle every nerve and watch your ecstasy,
the desire to talk about everything until the sun comes up

This is only being in love.
When being in love has burned away
love itself is not an easy road.

Are our roots so intertwined
that I could not imagine
being apart from you?

Hey! Let me ask you some questions!
Are you financially responsible and independent?
Do you want to have children?
Do you welcome Eastern and Western spirituality into your life?
Ok! Ok! Then how about creativity and passion?
Ok then, what are you doing Saturday night?

July 8, 2006
Inspired by the movie *Captain Corelli's Mandolin*

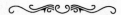

March 2010. My wife Loretta and I on our honeymoon in Mexico.

Fly with Me

Come fly with me

let us free-fall above the clouds
and find the stars

let us soar through our surface
and find what lies below

Come move with me

let us dance the pulse together
and hear our hearts

let us step into the unknown rhythm of tomorrow
and trust in the flow

May 7, 2006

August 2010. The prairie sky over Alberta.

In a Stranger's Face

Would you recognize the lines
In the face of a stranger

Would you hear the words
If we met in the market place

I was tasting the peaches with my eyes
Did you see me smiling

That was me in the baby's giggle
Little faces always shine true

I was walking in the flowers
In the arms of the tall man

I was there in the cute woman
The one with the green skirt

Yes, yes. You do recognize
The pulse all around

Do you see the divine

My soul shifts west
Across the setting sun
Lights move and shadows grow

What lives in the light
Follow the threads
Time, space, spirit
Portals grow

August 13, 2006

January 2009. Tibetan women walking around, as is tradition, the Dharmarajika Stupia that contain relics from Buddha at Sarnath, India.

I Was't There

I feel your heart
Little girl
Little boy

I know you needed
To be held
And told a thousand times
What a precious gift you are
But I wasn't there

I know you needed
To be tossed up into the air
And fly for an eternity
Until you landed safely in my arm
But I wasn't there

I know you needed
To hear sweet words
Of love, encouragement, and praise
Every day, every day
But I wasn't there

I know you needed
To be embraced
Held and cherished in the warmest way
Day and night
But I wasn't there

I know you needed
to be heard
to have your own voice
and to sing as often as you wanted
anytime you wanted
But I wasn't there

I know we children are divine
Children of light
Living in an infinite field of love
Every moment of every day
The divine will be there

Little boy, little girl
You will always be safe
You will always have a place
You are always cherished
Don't ever forget
You are a precious gift of God

October 4, 2006

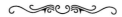

April 1971. My family just before we left Georgetown, Guyana, on our way to a new life in Canada. I was ten years old. My mother and my paternal grandmother are in the background.

A Sense of Wonder

Did you see the yellow butterfly
The one with black dots and shallow tail
Yey, yey that's the one

Do you remember the color of the leaves
On that tall maple beside the park
You know the one
Wow, the top leaves were a florescent orange
There were also yellow and red

Hey, what about the week old baby
Wasn't she beautiful
Seeing her amazing innocent eyes
Touched my soul
What about you
Did you see the divine in her eyes

What about the amazing music
Coming from the café
The fiddle and guitar
Resonated with my heart
The singer's voice
How angelic

Did you catch the aroma
Coming out of JJ Bean on Sixth Avenue
The fresh roasting coffee
How could you miss it
The pungent smell
Made me smile again

Did you use your sense of wonder today
And experience the miracles
All around us

October 21, 2006

August 2010. Flowers and plants from our rooftop garden in Vancouver.

If Children Were Our Teachers

Imagine if children were our teachers
Everything we do would be about playing

If you are sad, cry
If you are happy, laugh out loud

Use your imagination

Share
Eat with your whole body

Enjoy the sweet things
Spit out bitter things
Lick your plate

Look at the world with awe
Smile, do goofy things
Give hugs, say I love you
Jump in puddles
Dance

Sing silly songs
Stick your tongue out
Make funny faces
Speak your truth

Talk to strangers
Love animals
Smell flowers

Live for adventure
Fight and then make up
Be a superhero anytime
Be innocent

November 11, 2006

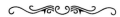

August 2010. Children playing near the farmer's market at Trout Lake,
Vancouver.

Dance the River of Life

Time is a river
Ebbing and flowing
What does one life mean?
Each choice opens
The path below our feet

Move in the flow
Dance the eternal dance
Dance the sperm
Moving in the gravity well
Of mother egg

Dance the infant
Pure and innocent
Follow the playground
Of childhood
Carefree
Full of sweet discovery

Dance the youth
Seek self
Who am I?
Test beyond the line
Find the solid ground
Stand up tall

Dance the woman
Shining and radiant
Give flow
Be the lifegiver
Paint the world
With a rainbow of beauty

Dance the man
strong, courageous
Be the shield and sword
Stand in the wind
Hold the ground

Dance the elder
Wise sage
Teach the world love
Dance the creation dance
Give the flow of life

Dance, dance the river of life.

December 31, 2006

January 2009. A classical Indian dancer performing a north Indian dance at Varanasi, India.

Passageway

I stand in the center
Looking out at the passageways.
Do you see the flow?
Invisible reality supporting me,
I have moved beyond the dark place—
The place of ignorance.

Stand in the light with me;
Let us follow the torchlight
Of knowledge and wisdom.
See the divine intelligence
Beyond limit.

Step outside the current;
No need to swim anymore—
SURRENDER.
Go to the deep place.
We can transcend this reality.
Once you step down the path,
You take one step,
The divine moves ten.

Step onto the path.
Move beyond the net.
See the open water.
Dive in and hear my heart.
Don't be seduced
By this garden of temporary pleasures;
Step onto the path to liberation.

September 15, 2008

January 2009. An ancient stone bridge on the way to the fort and palaces near Orcha, India.

Cosmic Lover

Come with me.
I will show you
The nothingness
The dark empty void.

See the darkness
Without eyes.
Surrender:
I give myself
To you.

Melt with me
Into the emptiness—
Vast unmanifested
Potential.

Surrender your thoughts.
Be insane.
Step over the edge.
Fall without expectations.

Open your heart.
Where is the illusion?
Pain is no more.
Love the fear.
Jump any way.

There is no you;
There is no I.
Witness the birth
Of the universe.

Time and space
Begin and end here
In our hearts.
Surf the energy waves.

Fall and know
That you will be supported.
Play and know no end.

Dance with Brahma.
Be the solar wind.
Dance the creation dance.
Look inside;
Ignite ten thousand suns.
Feel the ecstasy
Of birth.

Love with all your heart.
Feel every atom
Of your being dance.
Shake the universe;
Be the miracle
Of love.

October 31, 2007
After completing my first Illumination
Intensive Course

January 2009. Carving on the eastern group of temples at Khajuraho, India. Some of the carvings depict parts of the *Kama Sutra*.

Creation Dance

Breathe in stardust.
Breathe out atoms of being.
Shower the universe
With your love.

Dance with particles.
Dance the creation dance.
Move the cosmos
With your pulse.

Open your inner eye.
See the invisible.
Watch a flower
Open up.
See yourself
Reflected in golden petals.

See a bud.
Look deeper.
Can you see creation?
Feel the fire.

Follow a bee.
Watch her fly drunk
With Life's sweetness.
Fly with joy.

Hitch a ride
On an eagle's back.
See the world
With bigger eyes.
Look again.

Catch a wave
Behind a fish.
Follow the ripples.
Listen to the echo
Calling to you.

Drop the story
Of who you think you are.
It all means nothing.
Step into just being.
See the cosmic lovers dance.

October 31, 2007
After completing my first Illumination
Intensive Course

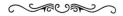

August 2008. A bumblebee on a wild flower at Mount Baker,
Washington State, USA.

Step over the Edge

Step over the edge;
Dare to be insane.
Fall down,
Fly free,
Feel the ground.

Choose to see invisible miracles;
Dance on the head of a pin
With *Streptococcus*.

Choose to be in the flow;
Swim in a drop of water
With *Paramecium*.

Choose connection
With everyone;
Surf the river of blood
Pumping in the heart of an enemy.

Hear the joy
In a baby's first cry;
Feel the surrender
In death's last breath.

Choose beauty
All around;
Fly on the back of a bumblebee.
Drink from a flower.

Push up through the ground
With a seed,
Becoming a grandmother cedar.

Float on the back of an eagle;
Change perspective.
See the world as one.

Surf the waves
On the tail of a humpback;
Dive the deep depths.

Soar on bubbles of laughter
With a child
Tossed into the air,
Free from gravity.

Chase the tail
Of a comet
Racing away from the sun;
Touch the edge of the universe.

Give up
On limitation;
Expand, expand.
Become nothing.
Be everything.

Dare to be insane;
See the unseen.
Fall deeply,
Madly in love.

March 2, 2008
Remembering my neighbour
Isobel Kiborn
(January 25, 1939-February 27, 2008)

July 2008. The view after I hiked to the top of Sulfur Mountain, Banff, Alberta.

The Gathering Place

Let me tell you of the gathering of men.
Like the great journey of the salmon
Following their ancient call,
Men gather.
Men put aside their daily toils,
Part from their families.
Preparations are made.
Fathers take their sons away
From their mothers
During the night.

Silently, through the darkness,
The river flows,
As sons and fathers move
Through the night.
The tide builds.
A purpose-filled journey begins.
The wheel turns.

Male spirit and soul propel strong feet.
Hear the call,
Powerful and primal.
YA WAY! YA WAY AHA!
YA WAY! YA WAY AHA!
YA WAY! YA WAY AHA!

Mountains cannot defeat
This river of feet.
Raging rivers,
Ice and snow
Nor storms
Can defeat
This river of feet.

Hunger, bleeding feet,
And pain
Only serve to test
This river of feet.
Hear the drumbeat
Of a thousand feet.

Like gathering blood
On its journey to the heart,
Men move to the gathering place
As journey-marked faces
Speak in communion.
The place by the river
Is marked by sweat,
By blood,
And by smoke.
Light from a universe of fires
Beckons in the night.

This is the place of renewal
And freedom.
This is a place of pain and joy.
This is a place of honor and courage.
This is a place of clarity and integrity.

Heroes gather here.
Sons look upon their fathers
With wide-eyed awe.
Sons know their fathers' love.
Sons look upon their fathers' actions.

Words are not needed.
A brotherhood of fire,
Of passion,
Of love,
Of joy
Is gathered here.

Over the course of days
Sons learn.
The male heart,
The legacy of men,
Nurturing the masculine flame,
Is renewed in this
Ancient gathering place.

Elders initiate men and teach the code,
Helping to purify and renew
The male spirit and soul
To prepare men for battles,
large and small.

Women, let your men go.
Hear the call, men,
Of the gathering place.

YA WAY! YA WAY AHA!
YA WAY! YA WAY AHA!
YA WAY! YA WAY AHA!

Hear the call, men,
Of the gathering place.

July 1997
Written for a men's gathering I led near Vancouver,
three years after doing my own men's weekend.

August 2006. Totem poles at an ancient Haida village on the Queen Charlotte in British Columbia.

The Great Tree

The wheels turn.
My body decays.
I look upon the stone
Where a tree grows.

I have become wood,
Leaves and flowers.
I dance
In the moonlit garden
With my father
And my father's father,
With my mother
And my mother's mother,
Reaching to the root.

See my connection?
I am that branch
On the great tree.
I have never been alone.

The wheel turns.
My playful laughter rises
In bubbles
Above the rain-soaked courtyard
Where a tree grows.

I shelter under the canopy.
Small fingers embrace
The tender smooth bark.
I play in the puddles,
Feeling my heart glow
Under my father's loving gaze.

I am the divine child
Born into a great house.
I am the living link on the great tree.

The wheel turns,
How can I doubt?
I can always dance
In the moonlit garden,
Play in the puddles in the courtyard.
I am bursting with love,
For the great tree
grows in me.

April 19, 2008

1950s. My mother's family is at the top and my father's family on bottom. In the top photo, my mother is on the far left beside my maternal grandparents. In the bottom photo, my father is in back row, second from the far left behind my paternal grandparents.

Prayer for a Goddess

Fields of wild rye
Golden strands
Glide past my bare skin.
My hands comb past
Scalp,
Warm skin,
Ears.

Is this madness
To touch
Stalks of grass
And feel you?

The sun-baked earth,
Rich and sensual,
Is your skin.
Sweet mysteries live here.

If I kissed the earth
Would you feel a tingle?
I am drunk with your scent
As flowers push up from your skin.
Your radiance
Dances in my eyes,
Red, pink, and purple.

Your tears of joy
Gather in deep cracks in the rock,
Cutting, babbling brooks.
As dragonflies dance
Their transformation dance,
Metamorphosis all around,
I am becoming
The light.

Once more
My open heart calls to yours.
Thunder echoes your heart;
The air is charged with your pulse.
I feel you surround me;
I surrender.
I feel you
Melt me.

Each step brings me
Close to you, my love.
My heart is open.
I walk through golden fields;
I feel you near.

Hear my prayer.

May 3, 2008

August 2010. My wife Loretta at a brunch to celebrate our wedding with her family in Saskatoon, Saskatchewan.

Dreams

Nymphs dance,
Drifting on creation winds,
Catching dreams,
Devouring them whole.

Manifestations big and small
Pulse electric.
Devas listen,
Waiting to serve.

Dance the transformation dance!
Be a dragonfly,
Play in the light,
Be the midsummer's morning.
Dream a new day.

Unzip this coat,
Lighten your heart,
Tell me your dreams.
No one but you
Holds the key.

How easy can it be?

May 10, 2008

January 2009. Sunset over the Ganga River at the Magh Mala festival, a
Hindu religious event, at Allahabad, India.

Mystery Meditation

I float
In a vast ocean of love
Warm
Totally supported

Floating
Floating

I float on an immense ocean of love
I surrender all thoughts
My thoughts are bubbles

Floating
Floating

I am surrounded
By a warm
Ocean of love

Floating
Floating

I let go
I surrender
I am infinite
I am light

Floating
Floating

I am floating in a vast
Ocean of love

May 11, 2008

चक्रमरा-स्थल

भगवान बुद्ध ने इस स्थान पर ध्यानस्थ चंक्रमरा
करते हुये तीसरा सप्ताह बिताया था। चबूतरे पर जो कमल
चिन्ह दिखलाई पड़ रहे हैं वे उन स्थानों का संकेत करते हैं
जहाँ चंक्रमरा करते हुए उनके चररा पड़े थे।

January 2009. Monks meditating outside the temple at Bodhgaya, India.

Two Wolves

Silver globe
Radiant goddess of the night
Reflects in glowing eyes

Keen ears
Silent paws
Move through the forest

My spirit dances
With glowing eyes and fur
Howling at the full moon

My vision shifts

Two wolves
Two different paths

One wolf
Walks alone
A worthy life
Exploring
The sweet mysteries of the night
The moon is my companion

My vision shifts

A second wolf
Shares the forest path
Purposeful steps
A family to feed and defend
A smoking fire
The moon catches echoes of my love

Which path?
Tell me spirit helper

May 17, 2008

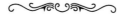

July 2009. Ancient pictographs on cliffs in the Stein Valley, British Columbia. Aboriginal people used this valley to initiate their young people.

A Fun, Family Lives Here

Step in
Bring your heart
This is a place to be real
All are welcome
A pot of warm tea awaits
And love-filled snacks invite
Come in and be nurtured

Children playing
Ripples of laughter
float on the air

Let go of your troubles
Speak and be heard
Feel the love
that you are meant to be

Activity buzzes all around
Howdy neighbor
Good to see you
A fun family lives here

May 30, 2008

March 2009. Loretta and my little brother dancing before my birthday
party started.

The Stars Are Watching

Look up.
Point of light.
Connect the dots.

Hear the message in the bottle.
We have been watching it all.

We watched from the time
you left the forest.
We watched when
you first walked upright.
We could see
your first fires.
We were the roof
as you danced into the night,
praising Father Sky and Mother Earth.
We have seen
your glorious monuments
rise and fall.

We watched as
you reached for the moon
with your technology.

We have also seen your wars.
We have seen your hate.
We have heard the lies.

It pains us to watch.
But then there is how you love.

In all of time,
we have never seen anything
like how you love.
The love of humankind
stops our tears.

How beautiful.
How crazy and impulsive.
How do you bear it?
What does it feel like
to have your heart glow
when you are near someone dear?
What is it like to give your heart
only to receive one back.

No need for demonstrations of devotion,
just a simple exchange.

We pray that you remember the miracle that is your love.

May 20, 2008
Inspired by the movie *Stardust*

July 2010. The sunset over Vancouver.

Worth Living For

What makes life worth living for you?
I live for beauty
To behold a field of wildflowers
On a mountaintop
On a warm spring day.
A rainbow of Red Indian paintbrush
Purple alpine lupine
White yarrow
Pink heather
My soul glows near beauty.

How wonderful to fall into the pools of light
In the eyes of a woman
Who knows herself
And feels at peace
A woman who knows her radiance
Let us drink each other's eyes.

Have you ever walked by a playground
And watched children playing?
I could float away
On the bubbles of laughter
Play and laughter
How beautiful!

What about a sunrise or sunset?
What a gift of colour
The hope of a new day
The gratitude for another day.

Grant me beauty
And I could live forever

I live for love,
romantic love.
To give my heart
To be in service
And feel another glow
Whenever we are near
To be consumed in passions flames
I give myself
Help me purify my soul.

There is also philial love
I've got your back, my friend
I'll be back with ammunition
Count on me
I'll be there
I will listen
And give you my truth
Mi casa es su casa, mi amigo.

I live for poetry
Sweet words
Caress my ears
Music for my heart and soul
Whitman, Thoreau, Frost, Service,
Bly, Rumi, Gibran, Hafiz.

Mystic magic
Incarnations of joy
Tales of love
Laments of pain and sorrow
Speak to my heart
May I live to contribute a verse
Give voice to my dreams
"Take the road less traveled"
"Suck out all the marrow."

Meet me in the field
Tell me tales of old
Imagine the possibilities.

I live for beauty
For love
For poetry
Grant me these three
Or take me out of this empty room!

June 20, 2008

July 2008. Hiking near Mount Baker, Washington State, USA.

Mermaid Dream

Warm sand underfoot,
Footprints etch my presence in nature's domain.
Water moved by unseen forces surges onto sand.
Rays from morning sun stir my emotions.

Up ahead on the beach.
What is it? What?
Something moves at waters' edge.
Is it human or not?
My eyes focus on the moving form.
Human, it's human!

A mermaid, human from the waist up,
Eyes blue as the sky,
Hair long and flowing,
Face not unlike Athena,
Sculptured arms, slender and graceful,
Breasts beautifully formed and smoothly curving.

My fingers gently touch her,
Mermaid no longer, her caressing hands return my touch.
Human instinct flows as two join,
Bodies exchange warmth,
Passion envelopes two forms at waters' edge.

Two bodies on the sand,
Human both, in natures domain.
Flesh touching flesh in total abandon,
Ritually exploring each other.
Energy endlessly consumed in the heat of passion's glow.

Footprints in the sand,
Water flowing around my feet,
A struggling fish flops on the beach.
Gently I return it to nature's domain.
The sky now sprinkled with colours
Takes the sun away.

May 9, 1984
Sunset on May 5 at Bayfield, Ontario

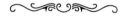

March 2008. The beautiful beach at Tulum, Mexico.

Four Little Paws

Icicle trees shimmer in the twilight.
Sculptured drifts move
as the north wind chills my face.
Four paw prints mark a trail.

I follow down the lane
in search of the little lost soul.
Her fur is thick, I hope.
The winds speak of a strong little heart
that they cannot chill.

Someone must love those four little paws
for the snows would have had her
were it not for the glow in her little heart.
Up ahead shadows move
as a door opens for four little paws.

January 1986

July 2010. A visit with our neighbour's two cats, Cardamom and Pepper, at our house.

Simple Love

Spring winds bring the rains.
Trees awaken from winter slumber.
Life renews itself all round.
Robin redbreasts hopping around.

The trill of spring songs echoes through the air
as if to say, "Wake up, wake up,
Spring is here! There's nothing to fear.
Winter is no more."

Robins sing their songs
calling to someone dear,
"I will, I will love you.
Yes, yes, I will love you.
I am strong and brave."

With the exchange of a worm
the hopping two become one.
A simple spring ritual,
The gesture of love being quite literal.

I yearn for simple love such as this,
Simple exchange of affections.
Alas, we humans suffer too many love complicating afflictions.

April 16, 1986
After a snowy London, Ontario winter.

March 2009. A beautiful spring day at Kitsilano Beach in Vancouver.

Portrait

I struggle to paint her essence
using words as my paint
and paper as my canvas.
An image dances elusively in my mind.

Her aura of simple beauty is highly charged.
Her Victorian elegance captivates me.
She is sitting at a dining table.
Over her left shoulder, her free spirit glows.
Above her right shoulder, green life is nurtured.

In her caring right hand, a drinking glass is held.
Her left hand rests earthwardly parallel.

A golden glow caresses her shoulders.
Courage projects from her heart.
Her feet firmly hold the ground.
Her simple silky hair flows behind her head and neck.
Light radiates from her soft angular cheeks.
Her intelligent nose separate inviting eyes.
A warm smile always shapes her lips.
Her ovate face begs to be touched.

1990

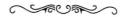

August 2010. Candid photo of Loretta relaxing with the newspaper at a café in Banff, Alberta.

Journeys

Your journey has brought you joy and pain
Bridges have been crossed
and storms weathered

Paths you have traveled
bear your footprints
but once

Though your feet may ache to retrace
the comfort of familiar sands
paths ahead promise only new joy and pain

Your feet may bleed
or they may be soothed
Remember however
that you must choose your own path

1986

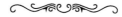

July 2009. Hiking in the Stein Valley, British Columbia.

Fly

Raven in the sky
Black
Sharp beak
Now on a birch tree
Way up high

Another friend calls
lands
calls again
Displacing raven to the sky

Darkness falls
Birch tree still
Ravens call to me
Take to the sky and fly

March 11, 1993
Langara Golf Course, Vancouver

July 2009. Nightly sunset flight of crows to their roosting trees toward the east, outside Vancouver.

Take Warning

Bird in the bush
Chirp, peck, flutter
Be still
Watch
Black-capped chickadee
No, no
Downy woodpecker
Tap, peck, shuffle
Calls again
Small
Sickly
A city bird
Must be the pollution
Sad
Take warning
Ecosystem in peril

March 11, 1993
Langara Golf Course, Vancouver

April 2009. A dead fur seal on the beach near Tofino, Vancouver Island in British Columbia.

Raven tree
Sentinel on guard
Quiet
Acid rains
Watching

Intruding metal
Choking smoke
Arrogant primate
Noise

Caw, caw
Exploding sky
Black wings
Raven tree no more
Watching

March 11, 1993
Langara Golf Course, Vancouver

July 2009. Raven on Mount Seymour, North Vancouver.

Weeping Earth
Darkened clouds

Burning tree
Smoking bush
Forest dying

Bright sun
Warming ice
Greenhouse near

Drying air
Clouds gone
Desert here

Secret light
Now a blight
Ozone fright

Weeping Earth
Crying

March 11, 1993
Langara Golf Course, Vancouver

January 2009. A dry riverbed in India.

Seed

Moonrise on wind-swept field
Stars dancing in crisp winter's night
Sculptured drifts move at my feet
As north wind chills my face

I ponder sleeping life
Frozen underfoot
Hidden by ice and snow

A moonlit icicle
Lies broken at my feet
Encasing a tiny seed
Sleeping life

Pondering this seed
I wonder
Is not love like a frozen seed
Thawed in hopes that it will grow

February 25, 1986

December 2008. A snowy day on Commercial Drive in Vancouver.

Smile

Nothing can beat it.
It blinds the sun.
It fills the room.
It connects hearts.

It comes in many forms.
Nervous smiles.
Friendly smiles.
Lots-of-teeth smiles.
Caring smiles.

A smile is universal.
It can heal.
It gives us hope.
Nothing can beat it.

Don't stop smiling.
You make me smile.

1988

January 2009. A Tibetan Buddhist monk on a pilgrimage at Bodhgaya, India.

Prejudice

Rippling wind on open field
Oak and maple side by side
Chattering of leaves as two converse.

Oak   Stretch your branch out further so we may touch.
Maple I must not!
Oak   I can't touch you by myself. You must reach your branch out
          further so we may touch.
Maple I am a maple and you an oak. What would the wind and forest
          say if we touch?

Oak   Do you have leaves to catch the sun?
          Do you have roots in the ground we two stand on?
          You shed your leaves in fall, just like me.
          We both sleep through the winter.
          We grow seeds to propagate our kind.
          You have branches that reach for the sky, just like me.
          We grow green in the summer warmth.
          You are a tree, just like me.

Maple We have stood together for many winters,
          you an oak and I a maple.
          We have shared warm summer breezes,
          but our leaves are of different shapes, you and I.
          You grow acorns and I maple keys.
          I give maple syrup in the fall; you do not.
          Our trunks grow differently, you and I.
          You have a rougher bark than I do.
          What would the oaks and maples say if we touch, you and I.

Oak   They chatter from the forest, not from our field.
             We share the same growth rings, you and I.
             We have stood side by side sharing the sun.
Maple   Yes, but what will the oaks and maples say.
Oak   We have been home to those who soar in the air.
             We helped each other when a branch was taken, causing pain.
Maple   Yes, but what will the oaks and maples say.
Oak   I can't reach further, you must do the rest.
Maple   Yes, but what will the oaks and maples say!

1984

October 2010. A field at the Westminster Abbey in Mission, British Columbia.

Winter's Breath

A damp breeze stirs the fallen leaves into the air,
Winter's breath looms near,
trees shed their green summer coats.
My heart aches to see them bare,
exposed to the icy winds.

Hearts, like trees, must shed their summer coats.
December snows and February storms will cover the land
Trees, like hearts, must sleep.
Sleep until spring rouses them.

My heart, summer was warm.
There was a beautiful rose,
starry nights, laughter, and sunshine,
two sharing candle light and wine,
a special time and space.
There were rainstorms and lost hope.
My heart, like the trees, has grown.

It is cold . . . time to sleep.
Winter's breath looms near.
Spring will come, I know.
Will my next summer have a rose?
Sleep . . . Sleep . . .

November 2, 1985
Goodbye to Rosemary

January 2007. Hiking on Dog Mountain in North Vancouver.

Beautiful Butterfly

For Loretta

Come and play with me,
beautiful butterfly.
Break free from your cocoon.
The winds await the caress
of your radiant wings.

Let us dance the moment
with the forest nymphs.
Let us catch the winds
and fan passion's flame.
Let us dream the dream,
one moment upon the next,
in the garden, floating,
on the ever-moving river of life.

December 20, 2008

August 2007. A butterfly resting on the floor of the tropical rainforest in Guyana.

Dance the Dream

For Loretta

Dance the dream
one moment upon the next.
When I have come to my end
I will be grateful
for every moment
lived well
with deep love
and reverence.

Moments of friendship
and talking for hours.

Fragrance
tastes of sweet, bitter, salty, and sour
soft gentle touch
inhaling the music of a loved ones' voice
wisdom lived
fear when stepping over the edge
wind on my face
wilderness feeding my soul
passion burning hot
laughter
children playing
cool water
knowing who I am
giving my unique gifts

I reflect now, before the end,
and resolve to live well.
On my gravestone will be written,
"He lived well
and gave it all.
1961-____ "

January 2009

January 2009. A Hindu yogi on an ancient stone bridge on the way to the fort and palaces near Orcha, India.

I watched the full moon
Set in the western sky while
Facing the fire-filled eastern sky this morning.

The divine feminine lovingly looking
Into the fiery heart of the sacred masculine
Sharing the sky.
This is the world at the beginning of time.

Imagine what we can create?
Our Love and Light joined
In a sacred field of endless possibility.

December 2, 2009
My engagement poem to my wife Loretta
On the day of the full moon

January 2009. Scene from Baghigata at a riverside temple at Rishikesh, India.

The Path

Remove your shoes,
follow the path.

Smile your radiance,
be in love.

Feel the petals underfoot,
Bless the path.
Dance with Buddha's flickering shadow.
Inhale the sacred light.
Catch the fire with your heart.

Purify yourself.
Surrender the ground you know.

Step onto the path less travelled.

December 4, 2009
Inspired by the sign on the door I hastily wrote
on the day I proposed to my wife Loretta

January 2009. Path up to caves where Buddha meditated after becoming
enlightened, near Rajgir, India